Original title:
Just for Today

Copyright © 2024 Swan Charm
All rights reserved.

Author: Aron Pilviste
ISBN HARDBACK: 978-9916-79-108-0
ISBN PAPERBACK: 978-9916-79-109-7
ISBN EBOOK: 978-9916-79-110-3

Echoes of the Minute

Ticking softly, time slips through,
Moments whisper, fleeting, true.
A heartbeat lost in twilight's grace,
Echoes linger in empty space.

The clock's hands dance, a timeless show,
Fleeting seconds, fast and slow.
In the stillness, shadows play,
Memories fade, then drift away.

Today's Silent Revelations

Morning dew on fragile leaves,
A whispered truth the stillness weaves.
Voiceless secrets, softly spoke,
In the space where silence woke.

The sun unfurls a golden seam,
Awakening thoughts, just like a dream.
With open hearts, we find our way,
In every dawn of a brand new day.

The Beauty of Ephemeral Things

Petals falling, soft and light,
Dancing gently in morning's bright.
Glances shared that quickly fade,
Moments lost, yet memory made.

Life's a shadow, fleeting and rare,
In its brevity, we find care.
Every smile, a spark that sings,
In the beauty of ephemeral things.

Just Another Hour

Time drifts softly, like a breeze,
Slipping through our hands with ease.
Just another hour, yet it gleams,
A tapestry of hopes and dreams.

In quiet corners, stories bloom,
Words unspoken fill the room.
As shadows stretch and silence calls,
We find ourselves in whispered halls.

Today's Fragile Moments

In the dawn's soft glow, we breathe,
Each second a gift, we weave.
Whispers of time, so fleeting,
In silence, our hearts are beating.

A laughter shared under the sun,
In fragile moments, we've begun.
Holding hands, we chase the light,
In this dance, our spirits bright.

The Pulse of the Present

Feel the heartbeat of today,
A rhythm that won't fade away.
Life unfolds in vibrant hues,
A tapestry of endless views.

In every breath, we find our song,
In the now, we all belong.
Moments merge in sweet embrace,
In time's flow, we find our place.

A Dance of Fleeting Times

Twirl with shadows on the ground,
Echoes of laughter all around.
A moment glimmers, then it goes,
In the dance, our essence flows.

Step by step, we twine and sway,
With every heartbeat, night and day.
A fleeting glance, a whisper near,
Together, we conquer fear.

Serene Interludes

In quiet places, we can find,
A peace that smooths the troubled mind.
Gentle moments, soft and slow,
In stillness, our spirits grow.

Underneath the starlit skies,
Whispers of dreams begin to rise.
A tranquil heart can understand,
The beauty held in silent land.

Fleeting Seconds

Time whispers softly, fleeting dreams,
Moments flicker like sunlit beams.
A heartbeat passes, soft and slight,
Life's tapestry woven in the night.

We chase the shadows, grasp at air,
Holding on tightly, unaware.
Each second dances, swift and rare,
A waltz of time, beyond compare.

In laughter's echo, in tears that flow,
We treasure the now, let the past go.
With each tick tock, we softly sigh,
In the race of time, we live, we fly.

In the Heart of a Moment

In the heart of a moment, time stands still,
Breath held tightly, against our will.
Whispers of dreams linger in the air,
Caught in a gaze, a tender stare.

A heartbeat skips, yet all is clear,
Fleeting but lasting, we draw near.
Embraced by silence, the world fades away,
In this quiet space, we long to stay.

Time melts softly, like candlelight,
Every second savored, a pure delight.
In the heart of the moment, we take flight,
Creating forever, in our own night.

Cherished Light

In the gentle glow of evening's grace,
We find ourselves in a sacred space.
Cherished light wraps us like a shawl,
A golden embrace that calms us all.

As shadows lengthen, stories unfold,
In whispered tones, dreams are told.
Each glance exchanged, a treasure bright,
In the tender hues of cherished light.

Time slips quickly, yet we remain,
Basking in warmth, free of pain.
With hearts aglow, our spirits rise,
Under the canvas of starlit skies.

The Gift of This Minute

The gift of this minute, rare and true,
Wrapped in laughter, touched by you.
Breath of existence, sweet and light,
A pause in the chaos, pure delight.

Moments like treasures, cherished and dear,
In the hush of this minute, you are near.
With eyes that sparkle like stars at play,
We seize the magic, come what may.

Time's gentle rhythm, a dance so fine,
In the gift of this minute, your heart intertwines.
Together we weave, in joy, in pain,
In every heartbeat, love shall remain.

Today's Unraveled Threads

Each moment weaves a tale,
Colors bright and shadows pale.
With every stitch a story told,
A tapestry of dreams unfolds.

But threads may fray, and knots appear,
We tug at fears, we hold them near.
Yet in unraveling, we find our way,
A new design to greet the day.

In laughter's weave and sorrow's seam,
Life's fabric pulses, a vivid dream.
We gather strands of joy and pain,
Creating beauty where loss has lain.

As sun sets down to earth's embrace,
Old threads give way, new hopes replace.
In twilight's glow, our spirits soar,
A promise made, forevermore.

The Stillness of This Hour

In the hush, time seems to pause,
Nature whispers, without cause.
The world slows, and I breathe deep,
In this silence, secrets keep.

Soft shadows play on walls of light,
Stars prepare for the coming night.
With every heartbeat, calm descends,
In stillness, every worry mends.

The trees sway gently, a lullaby,
Moonlight dances, a silent sigh.
In this sacred space, I feel it clear,
The heart's true voice, so close and near.

Time stretches, a gentle hands,
In the glow, the universe stands.
Whispers of hope float in the air,
In this stillness, I feel you there.

A Snapshot of Tomorrow's Dreams

In the canvas of my mind,
Visions vivid and intertwined.
Skies painted with hues of hope,
In this dream, I learn to cope.

Mountains rise, and rivers flow,
Paths unknown begin to show.
Each step forward, a daring leap,
In these dreams, my heart will keep.

Faces of loved ones, bright and clear,
In every smile, warmth draws near.
Laughter echoes, futures bright,
A snapshot captured in pure light.

I reach for stars, I touch the night,
In dreams, I soar, I take flight.
Tomorrow's promise, I hold tight,
In the depths of dreams, I find my light.

Today's Simple Blessings

The sun peeks through the trees,
A gentle breeze brings ease.
Birds sing sweet melodies,
Nature's gifts, oh how they please.

A cup of tea in hand,
Moments quiet and grand.
Laughter shared with friends,
A warmth that never ends.

A child's smile so bright,
Stars twinkling at night.
Books that take you far,
Finding joy where you are.

The scent of blooming flowers,
Quiet time in the hours.
Grace in each little thing,
Grateful hearts always sing.

In the chaos, find the pause,
In the smallness, feel the cause.
Simple blessings every day,
In our hearts, they gently stay.

A Flash of Clarity

In a moment, all is clear,
Fears fade away, disappear.
Thoughts that once felt heavy,
Lift like clouds, no longer edgy.

A truth revealed so bright,
Guides us through the night.
Worries quiet, peace ignites,
Inspiration takes its flight.

Amidst the shadows, we see,
The path to who we can be.
With courage born anew,
Every challenge we'll pursue.

Wisdom's whisper, soft yet loud,
Lost in thought, now feels so proud.
Choices made with open hearts,
Through the dark, we find new starts.

In the stillness, we awake,
Every fear begins to break.
A flash of light that shows the way,
Hope's reminder in the day.

Here in the Stillness

Soft whispers of the night,
Stars shimmering with light.
The world outside is calm,
Here, I find my balm.

In the quiet, thoughts flow,
Slowly, gently, they grow.
Emotions weave and blend,
A time to reflect and mend.

Shadows dance upon the wall,
Echoes of a once loud call.
Breathing deep, I feel alive,
In this stillness, I thrive.

Memory's tender embrace,
Filling up the empty space.
Understanding starts to bloom,
In the depth of darkened rooms.

Here in the stillness, I learn,
Every flame can brightly burn.
Peace resides within my core,
Finding strength forevermore.

A Soft Step Forward

With each step, the ground I feel,
A gentle shift, a quiet reel.
Forward we move with grace,
Faith in every trace.

Whispers of hope guide me on,
Singing soft like a dawn.
In the unknown, I find my way,
Courage grows day by day.

Through the fog, a glimpse appears,
Washing away deep-seated fears.
Each heartbeat leads, a steady beat,
With patience, I meet each feat.

Softly treading, I embrace,
Moments cherished in this space.
With every breath, a chance to grow,
In the journey, I will flow.

Life unfolds in tender light,
With every step, I'm in flight.
Forward I move, unwavering and bold,
In this journey, treasures unfold.

Here Lies Contentment

In the quiet of the night,
Whispers drift, soft and light.
Beneath the stars, dreams take flight,
Here lies peace, pure delight.

Simple pleasures pave the way,
Golden rays of a new day.
In laughter shared, worries stray,
Here lies joy, come what may.

Fields of green where flowers bloom,
Scent of earth in nature's room.
In gentle winds, life finds its tune,
Here lies love, dispelling gloom.

Moments cherished, time stands still,
Heartbeats echo with will.
In every smile, a promise thrills,
Here lies hope, a sacred fill.

Underneath a sky so wide,
Embracing life, a tender guide.
In every heart, we must confide,
Here lies warmth, walking beside.

A Thread through Time

Weaving tales of days gone by,
Threads of laughter, moments shy.
In every stitch, a memory high,
A tethered heart, a boundless sky.

The echoes of the past still sing,
Whispers of love that time will bring.
In each heartbeat, a timeless ring,
A thread through time, life's offering.

Gentle hands that hold the lore,
Stories shared behind closed door.
In every glance, what came before,
A thread through time, forevermore.

Footsteps carved in ancient stone,
Each a story, each a bone.
In the silence, we feel the tone,
A thread through time, never alone.

Seasons shift, yet still we find,
Fragments of dreams left intertwined.
In the fabric, our lives aligned,
A thread through time, fate defined.

The Pulse of the Present

A heartbeat echoes in the still,
Moments gather, time to fill.
In the now, we drink our fill,
The pulse of life, a steady thrill.

Sunlight dances on our skin,
Every breath, a chance to begin.
In the tapestry, woven thin,
The pulse of now, where we win.

Waves of laughter, joy cascades,
In the shadows, fears do fade.
In this presence, life parades,
The pulse of heart, never jade.

Time unwinds with gentle grace,
In every glance, a warm embrace.
In the chaos, we find our place,
The pulse of love, a sacred space.

Each moment, a treasure to keep,
In the quiet, dreams we reap.
In every heartbeat, memories leap,
The pulse of now, a promise deep.

In the Embrace of Now

Time suspends in sacred air,
In the moment, we find care.
With open hearts, we choose to share,
In the embrace, our souls lay bare.

Gift of life in fleeting shades,
In the laughter, joy cascades.
Each tender touch, a bond persuades,
In the embrace, time never fades.

Whispered secrets, soft and low,
In the stillness, feelings flow.
With each heartbeat, love will grow,
In the embrace, we let it show.

Paths converging under stars,
In unity, we break our bars.
With every dream, we travel far,
In the embrace, we're never marred.

Wrapped in warmth, the world feels right,
In this moment, pure and bright.
With open arms, we hold the light,
In the embrace, our spirits ignite.

Grounded in the Now

In the stillness, I breathe deep,
Moments linger, secrets to keep.
Nature whispers, soft and clear,
Here in this moment, I find my cheer.

Leaves are dancing, shadows play,
Time stands still, melting away.
The sun dips low, the sky ablaze,
Caught in the beauty, lost in the gaze.

Footfalls echo on the ground,
In each heartbeat, life is found.
Every choke of sadness, passed
Embraced by now, a love that lasts.

As the day fades into night,
Stars emerge, a gentle light.
Gratitude fills my weary soul,
Grounded in this moment, I am whole.

Today's Quiet Spark

Morning bleeds in soft and bright,
Promises wrapped in soft sunlight.
A quiet moment before the rush,
Within this peace, I feel the hush.

Birds are singing, calm descends,
Hope rekindles as daylight bends.
In every smile and every part,
The world ignites a quiet spark.

Time flows gently, echoes loud,
Thoughts meander, unbowed.
Within stillness, dreams awake,
Creating paths that hearts can take.

Each tick of the clock a gentle nudge,
Inviting me to slip and plunge.
Today's a canvas, blank and bright,
Filled with whispers, pure delight.

Moments Wrapped in Time

Each tick dances with the past,
Memories twinkle, shadows cast.
In the fabric of the day,
Moments weave in bright array.

Gentle laughter, a quick embrace,
Time stands still in this warm place.
Captured glances, stories told,
Heartfelt treasures, pure as gold.

As seconds fade, they leave behind,
Fragments of heart, eternally entwined.
Caught in the tapestry we weave,
Moments echo, we believe.

With every breath, a chance to grow,
In the current, I learn to flow.
Yesterday's whispers guide me true,
I am wrapped in me and you.

The Joys of This Hour

Sipping tea on a gentle breeze,
Joy unfurls with such sweet ease.
Time slips softly through my hands,
In this hour, my heart expands.

The world outside, a distant hum,
In quiet corners, wonders come.
Each moment holds a hidden glee,
A fleeting glance, my spirit free.

Golden sunsets paint the sky,
With every breath, I learn to fly.
The joys of now, so rich and pure,
In this hour, my soul finds cure.

With every laugh, a sound divine,
Moments shared, like sparkling wine.
Embrace the now, let worries cease,
In the joys of this hour, I find peace.

Threads that Bind the Now

In whispers soft, the moments sway,
We weave our tales, the night and day.
Each glance a thread, a line untold,
In present's grasp, our hearts unfold.

Like colors bright that blend and mix,
We stitch our love with gentle tricks.
The tapestry of joy and tears,
Each stitch a fight against our fears.

The laughter shared, a golden seam,
In memories spun, we live our dream.
Through trials faced, we find our way,
In every stitch, the light's array.

Let not the future tear apart,
These woven threads that hold the heart.
In present's embrace, we shall find,
The endless ties that love has lined.

Through every moment's gentle pull,
Our dreams expand, our hearts are full.
Together we walk, side by side,
In threads that bind, we shall abide.

A Portrait of the Present

A canvas bright, with colors bold,
Each stroke a story waiting to be told.
In hues of laughter, shades of pain,
We paint our lives, in sun and rain.

The brush of time, it moves so swift,
Each fleeting moment, a precious gift.
In every glance, a light to see,
The portrait held in memory.

Beneath the layers, secrets hide,
In each embrace, the world confides.
The vivid scenes through which we roam,
In every heart, we find our home.

With every twist, the canvas grows,
Our lives entwined, like vines that close.
In present's art, we find our grace,
A masterpiece of time and space.

So let us craft, with gentle hands,
A world of beauty, where love stands.
In vibrant strokes, let us express,
The portrait of the present's bless.

Intimacy with the Immediate

In moments small, the heart expands,
A gentle touch, a warm embrace.
The time we share, a soft command,
In every glance, a sacred space.

The laughter dances through the air,
In whispers sweet, we come alive.
Together here, no room for care,
With open hearts, our spirits thrive.

The fleeting seconds, pure and true,
In every breath, a promise made.
With you, my love, I find my view,
In moments shared, our fears allayed.

In sips of tea, in quiet sighs,
We find our truth, in small delights.
In every heartbeat, fate implies,
The now is where our love ignites.

So let us stay, in present's hold,
With every heartbeat, secrets told.
Intimacy blooms, a fragrant flower,
In moments brief, we find our power.

Reflections in a Hasty Stream

The river flows, a swift parade,
In currents strong, our stories fade.
With every splash, a memory wakes,
In hasty depths, the heart still aches.

The ripples dance, a fleeting chance,
To catch a glimpse, a broken glance.
In swirling tides, our hopes are tossed,
In streams of time, we face the lost.

Yet clarity finds a way to shine,
In fleeting moments, the world divine.
Each wave that breaks, a truth unmasked,
In reflections clear, our hearts are tasked.

As we navigate this rushing flow,
We'll forge our path, let courage grow.
In every turn, a chance to see,
The beauty found in you and me.

So breathe it in, this messy dream,
In every turn, love's soothing beam.
Through rushing waters, we shall gleam,
In reflections pure, our spirits beam.

A Quiet Promise

In the hush of dawn's light,
Whispers of hope take flight.
Softly the heart vows to be,
A beacon of love, wild and free.

Beneath the stars' gentle glow,
Silent dreams begin to grow.
A pact with the night, so profound,
In stillness, this promise is found.

With each step upon the sand,
I hold the vows close at hand.
Trust in the path yet unknown,
In quietude, seeds are sown.

Through the storms, through the rain,
This promise will not wane.
For in the heart's sacred chamber,
Resides a quiet, eternal ember.

In every moment, soft and bright,
A promise rests in the night.
Each breath, a gentle reminder,
Of love that grows, ever kinder.

Today's Simple Joy

Sunlight dances on the grass,
Moments fleeting, yet they last.
The laugh of a child, pure delight,
Makes the ordinary feel just right.

With a cup of warm tea, I sit,
Savoring life's little bits.
Birds sing sweetly, a soft tune,
As I bask beneath the afternoon moon.

The world slows down, time stands still,
In these moments, I find my will.
A flower blooms, colors so bright,
Nature's canvas, pure delight.

With every breeze that softly blows,
A whisper of peace gently flows.
It's in today, joy starts to unfold,
In simple moments, stories told.

Hand in hand, with friends nearby,
We share the laughter, the soft sigh.
Today's simple joys, we embrace,
In every heartbeat, we find our place.

The Art of Stillness

In the quiet of the early morn,
Serenity is born.
With every breath, I find my way,
To the heart of the day.

The world spins fast; I pause to see,
The beauty that surrounds me.
A moment taken, a still embrace,
Cultivating peace in this space.

Thoughts like clouds drift on by,
Yet here I sit, no rush, no try.
In stillness, answers begin to flow,
A gentle knowing, soft and slow.

Every sigh carries the weight of grace,
In this quiet, I find my place.
A canvas blank, waiting for light,
The art of stillness feels so right.

With the world outside in a flurry,
I find my calm in this hurry.
Embracing silence, I feel so free,
In the art of stillness, I simply be.

Today's Unfolding

As dawn breaks with a gentle sigh,
New possibilities start to fly.
With every ray that warms the ground,
In today's unfolding, joy is found.

Secrets hidden in morning's breath,
Life whispers softly, conquering death.
Each moment brings a chance anew,
In open hearts, dreams break through.

Nature's palette, vibrant and pure,
Each color reflects a heart's allure.
With open arms, I greet the day,
In today's unfolding, I find my way.

The tangled threads of fate invite,
As I dance under the tender light.
Each step a promise, each glance a spark,
In simple wonders, I leave my mark.

With laughter shared and stories spun,
In today's unfolding, we are one.
Embracing the now, we set it free,
In every heartbeat, life's melody.

With the Winds of Change

Whispers in the air, they call,
Roots that tremble, but stand tall.
Seasons shifting, heart in dance,
Life unfurls, a daring chance.

Clouds that gather, skies that shift,
In their midst, a hopeful gift.
Paths once clear, now winding round,
In each turn, new hope is found.

Leaves that rustle, stories shared,
In the tempest, hearts have bared.
Change is but a gentle friend,
Bringing light that will not end.

With each breath, embrace the shift,
Each new moment, nature's gift.
Sail through storms, with courage bold,
In the winds, let dreams unfold.

Trust the journey, wild and free,
With the change, we learn to be.
Life's a canvas, colors blend,
In the winds, we find our mend.

Today's Unseen Grace

In the quiet of the morn,
Petals greet the world, reborn.
Softly shines the light of day,
Guiding hearts along the way.

Moments pass like fleeting streams,
Hidden beauty in our dreams.
Every smile, a silent song,
In the rush, we still belong.

Gentle whispers in the air,
Tell of love, beyond compare.
In the little things, we find,
Grace that warms the seeking mind.

Each embrace, a tender touch,
Reminds us we are loved so much.
In the chaos, pause, and see,
Today's grace sets our souls free.

Lift your gaze, let worry blend,
In this moment, hearts will mend.
For the unseen grace is near,
In each heartbeat, hold it dear.

This Serene Space

Here in quiet, moments blend,
Time suspends, and hearts intend.
Soft the light that gently flows,
In this space, serenity grows.

Whispers of the trees around,
Nature's peace, a gentle sound.
In the stillness, spirits soar,
Find your heart, and seek no more.

Clouds above a tranquil sea,
Reflect the deep serenity.
Each new breath, a calming wave,
In this space, our hearts are brave.

Moments stretch like endless skies,
In their depth, our spirit flies.
Here we gather, dreams in hand,
From this space, we understand.

Let the quiet fill your mind,
In this haven, peace you'll find.
For within this sacred place,
We can feel life's warm embrace.

Embracing the Now

Time rolls on, yet here we stand,
In the moment, hold my hand.
Every heartbeat echoes loud,
In this instant, we're so proud.

Let the past drift far away,
In the present, here we stay.
With each breath, our worries cease,
In the now, we find our peace.

Shadows fade with the rising sun,
Every second, we are one.
In the laughter, in the tears,
Here together, face our fears.

Capture joy, let sadness flow,
Every moment helps us grow.
With our hearts wide open, free,
Embracing all, just you and me.

So let time dance, let life sway,
In the now, we find our way.
With every glance, a love we sow,
Together here, embracing flow.

Today's Small Wonders

A dewdrop clings to grass,
Reflecting morning light.
The world hums a soft tune,
In the hush of dawn's flight.

Birds chirp from the boughs,
Each note a sweet delight.
A flower blooms in silence,
Nature's art, pure and bright.

Children laugh in the park,
Joy swims in sunlit air.
Miracles in the mundane,
Life's canvas, rich and rare.

A stranger's warm smile shared,
An act so simple, kind.
In these small wonders found,
Connection heart and mind.

Take a moment to see,
The beauty that surrounds.
Each day is a treasure,
In small wonders, joy abounds.

A Peaceful Interlude

The clock ticks slow and soft,
Time pauses, breath held tight.
A moment carved in stillness,
Beneath the starry night.

Candle flames dance gently,
Shadows play on the wall.
Whispers of the quiet,
In solitude's gentle call.

A cup of warm tea waits,
Steam spirals, fades away.
Thoughts drift like soft clouds,
In this haven, I stay.

The world outside subsides,
With all its rush and race.
Here in this sacred space,
I find my peaceful place.

Listen to the silence,
Feel it wrap around me.
In this calm interlude,
I embrace tranquility.

Savoring the Present

Birds flit through the green leaves,
Sun warms my upturned face.
Each breath a fragrant moment,
In this vibrant, lovely space.

The scent of blooming lilacs,
A dance of colors bright.
Life unfolding before me,
In the tender morning light.

With every bite of fruit,
Sweetness lingers on my tongue.
Memories sweetly woven,
In this song, life is sung.

Laughter shared with friends near,
Time seems to pause and bend.
Every second is precious,
As I savor, heart to mend.

In the rush of days gone by,
I choose to linger here.
In the now, I find joy,
Savoring all, oh so dear.

Threads of a Brief Time

Moments stitch together time,
A tapestry unfolds.
Each thread a unique story,
Soft secrets to be told.

Laughter floats in warm air,
Echoes of joy and pain.
Threads of love and longing,
Woven in hope, not in vain.

The rustle of old pages,
A book of memories past.
Each chapter, a glimpse shared,
In a journey unsurpassed.

Sunsets paint the horizon,
Colors fade to twilight's call.
Threads of a brief existence,
In the fabric, we are all.

Time is fleeting, yet holds true,
In the hearts of those we find.
Threads connect us, weaving life,
In the shared tapestry of mind.

Seeds of Today's Dreams

In the soil of our hopes, we plant,
Tiny seeds in the gentle earth.
Nurtured by passions that slant,
They blossom into visions of worth.

Whispers of future, we hear them call,
As we water with care and embrace.
Time dances lightly, never too tall,
Each moment a step in our chase.

Under the sky where the sun beams bright,
We toil with love in the warm light.
Every dream grows through day and night,
With roots that connect us, hold tight.

From the dawn to the twilight glow,
Our dreams take flight, vibrant and true.
With every heartbeat, the spirits flow,
Crafting a world meant for me and you.

Let us gather the dreams we've sown,
In fields of potential, let them spread.
For from the tiniest seeds we've grown,
A garden of hope lies ahead.

Embracing the Here and Now

The clock ticks softly, moments glide,
Let's cherish the breath we take now.
In this stillness, our hearts collide,
Time whispers secrets as they allow.

In laughter shared, in silence sweet,
We find our essence wrapped in grace.
Each fleeting beat brings us complete,
As memories linger, time we embrace.

The sun fades gently over the hill,
Colors blend in a brilliant array.
In every heartbeat, we feel a thrill,
Alive in this moment, come what may.

Let not tomorrow pull at our minds,
Or worries of yesterday break through.
We are the canvas, where life unwinds,
In colors bright, our spirits renew.

So hold this moment, feel it alive,
Let your heart be open and free.
In the now, we learn how to thrive,
In the here and now, just let it be.

Holding the Instant Close

A moment captured, crystal clear,
Like a firefly dancing in the night.
We hold it gently, lest it disappear,
A precious gem, a fleeting light.

In laughter shared and whispers low,
We find the magic that time can steal.
Each second a treasure, let it flow,
In the warmth of love, we truly feel.

The heartbeat quickens when we pause,
To savor the beauty in our grasp.
In every breath, there's a tender cause,
To hold the instant, a gentle clasp.

So gather the fragments of this time,
Embrace the sweetness, let it stay.
For in this heartbeat, life's true rhyme,
We find forever in the briefest play.

Let the echoes linger in our soul,
As we cherish what the moments give.
For in each instant, we become whole,
Learning to love, learning to live.

A Breath of Briefness

Inhale the softness of the breeze,
Moments that flicker, gentle and light.
A breath that carries all our pleas,
Whispers of dreams, taking flight.

In brevity's dance, life twirls around,
Each precious second slips through our hands.
But in this fleeting, joy is found,
As we weave through time's shifting sands.

Like dandelions caught in the air,
Floating freely, no burdens to hold.
In every sigh, a chance to repair,
Turning the fleeting into gold.

So pause and savor the tiny hues,
A sunset painted in amber glows.
In the briefness, there's nothing to lose,
Just moments that blossom like flowers that grow.

For time may wane, but we will know,
That each breath has its own sweet song.
In the rhythm of life, let love flow,
Grasping the briefness, where we belong.

A Moment's Whisper

In shadows soft, the whispers play,
A fleeting touch, by night or day.
The silence wraps around the heart,
As time unfolds, we drift apart.

Yet echoes linger, gently still,
A breath of hope, a quiet thrill.
We close our eyes, and then we see,
The beauty found in memory.

Each fragile word, a world anew,
Carried forth by morning dew.
Embrace the fleeting, hold it tight,
For moments pass like stars at night.

In every glance, a story told,
The warmth of love, the touch of gold.
A moment's whisper, soft and clear,
Calls us back, it draws us near.

So treasure each, let none escape,
In life's great book, we write our shape.
With every breath, we're here, we're now,
In whispered moments, we avow.

Treading Lightly Through Time

With every step, the earth we kiss,
A dance with time, a fleeting bliss.
In gentle paths where silence flows,
We thread the past that onward goes.

The sun sets low, we feel its glow,
Reminders of the paths we know.
In shadows long, the stories weave,
Each footfall whispers, learn, believe.

Among the trees, where secrets lie,
We wander forth, just you and I.
In nature's arms, we softly tread,
Through silent woods where dreams are bred.

The river's song, a tranquil guide,
As moments linger, drift and slide.
With each heartbeat, time's gentle flow,
Reminds us, oh, how far we've grown.

So tread with care, yet boldly roam,
In sacred spaces, find your home.
For life's a dance, a timeless rhyme,
As we tread lightly through the time.

The Choice of Now

In every heartbeat, worlds collide,
The choice of now, where dreams abide.
Each moment shines, a spark divine,
Awakening the soul's design.

We stand at crossroads, paths in view,
Each option waits, a chance so true.
With courage bold, we take a stand,
Creating futures, hand in hand.

Each breath a chance, each choice a gift,
In present's arms, our spirits lift.
No shadows linger, pasts undone,
For here we bloom, in morning sun.

With clarity, we see the light,
The choice of now, a guiding flight.
So seize the day, and let love flow,
For life unfolds in the choice of now.

Let worries fade, let fears release,
In every choice, discover peace.
Tomorrow's veil is yet unspun,
Embrace this moment, love has won.

Breathing in the Present

Inhale the joy, exhale the past,
A tranquil moment, breathing fast.
With every breath, we find our peace,
In present's hold, our worries cease.

The here and now, a sacred place,
We find our footing, we find our grace.
With open hearts, we take it in,
The gift of now, where life begins.

The world unfolds in vibrant hues,
With every breath, we choose, we choose.
The whispers call, the moments rise,
A symphony beneath the skies.

In stillness deep, our spirits soar,
Breathing in love, we crave for more.
So cherish each, let blessings flow,
For life, it sings, in the present glow.

With gratitude, we linger here,
In every breath, we shed our fear.
Together we stand, in peace profound,
Breathing in the present, love unbound.

Ephemeral Embrace

In twilight's soft embrace we find,
Moments whispered, sweet and kind.
Fleeting dreams dance on the air,
Promises made but never bare.

Warmth of laughter, lingering light,
Shadows blend with the approaching night.
Every touch, a fleeting spark,
Love's soft glow against the dark.

Memories fade like morning dew,
Yet in hearts, they stay so true.
Holding close what we can't keep,
In this fleeting joy, we leap.

Life, a canvas, swiftly drawn,
Colors bright before they're gone.
Embracing moments, sweet and rare,
For in the now, love fills the air.

Time's Gentle Gifts

Time whispers secrets to the trees,
Moments drift like autumn leaves.
Each second wrapped in golden thread,
In silence, stories softly spread.

Gentle glow of morning light,
Guides our hearts to take flight.
Each breath a treasure, pure and sweet,
Life's kindness found in each heartbeat.

Yet shadows linger on the way,
Marking moments that won't stay.
In the quiet, we must glean,
What it means to live, to dream.

Time's embrace is soft yet swift,
Every heartbeat, a precious gift.
Cherish the fleeting, hold it tight,
In love's deep well, we find our light.

Fleeting Shadows of the Hour

Fleeting shadows dance and play,
As daylight fades and slips away.
Moments lost in twilight's gleam,
Tangled thoughts, like a dream.

Whispers of dusk call our names,
In soft hues and gentle flames.
Each heartbeat marks the passing day,
Like footprints slowly washed away.

Time, a river, swift and strong,
Carries us along the song.
Hold on tight, let not the hour
Fade like petals, losing power.

In the dusk, we find our fate,
Seizing joy before too late.
Though shadows stretch and then depart,
Their lingering warmth fills the heart.

Steps in the Sunlight

Steps in the sunlight, warm and bright,
Pathways glimmer, pure delight.
Each footfall echoes in the day,
Guiding us along our way.

Laughter dances on the breeze,
Moments cherished, hearts at ease.
In shadows cast, our dreams take flight,
Chasing the dawn, embracing light.

With every stride, we weave a tale,
Of summer's whispers, soft and frail.
In the glow of the afternoon,
Our souls awaken, free as the moon.

Hand in hand, we wander far,
Under the gaze of a watching star.
For in each step, we live, we learn,
In sunlight's embrace, our spirits burn.

In This Instant

Time slows down, a gentle pause,
We gather dreams, in silent cause.
The world feels vast, yet close at hand,
In this instant, we understand.

Moments blend, a tapestry bright,
Stars whisper softly, through the night.
Each heartbeat echoes, a rhythmic dance,
In this instant, we take a chance.

The fleeting clouds above us drift,
Carrying with them, a precious gift.
In the stillness, the truth unfolds,
In this instant, our spirit holds.

A lover's gaze, a child's laughter,
The sweet embrace of now and after.
Here we stand, both lost and found,
In this instant, love abounds.

So breathe it in, this fragile time,
Where every moment can feel like rhyme.
In the quiet, let your heart sing,
In this instant, we are everything.

A Breath Between Heartbeats

In silence lies a world unknown,
A breath between, the space we've grown.
Time holds its breath and drifts away,
In this pause, we dare to sway.

Moments linger, then softly fade,
A dance of shadows, serenely laid.
In the stillness, we find our way,
A breath between, night swallows day.

Hope flickers bright, a candle's flame,
Voices whisper, calling our name.
In the quiet, each thought takes flight,
A breath between, we find our light.

Memory echoes a distant sigh,
An open window, the night sky high.
With every heartbeat, dreams revive,
A breath between, we feel alive.

So cherish this, the fleeting grace,
In every pause, we find our place.
In the space where we truly feel,
A breath between, the heart's appeal.

The Grace of the Present

In the present, moments weave,
Time's gentle thread, never to leave.
Sunlight spills on the golden ground,
The grace of now, in peace is found.

Whispers of wind, caress the trees,
Nature's melody, a soft breeze.
Here in the stillness, worries dissolve,
The grace of now, our hearts evolve.

Rays of laughter, echoes of joy,
In every heartbeat, hope to deploy.
Capture the fleeting, hold it tight,
The grace of now, a pure delight.

Every glance a promise made,
In the now, our fears outweighed.
With open arms, we embrace life's flow,
The grace of now, where love will grow.

So dance in this, the fleeting light,
Every second, a shared insight.
In the present, our souls ignite,
The grace of now, forever bright.

Here and Now

Underneath the sky so wide,
In this moment, dreams reside.
Leaves are rustling, whispers low,
Here and now, we let love flow.

The world spins fast, but we are still,
Time unfurls, a gentle thrill.
In laughter's glow and silence deep,
Here and now, our souls shall leap.

Clouds pass by, like fleeting thoughts,
In this stillness, the battle fought.
The heart reminds, with every beat,
Here and now, life's rhythm sweet.

Softly spoken, a word of grace,
Each moment cherished, no time to waste.
In the embrace of all that's true,
Here and now, it's me and you.

So take a breath, kiss the air,
In the present, without a care.
In every heartbeat, love's avow,
Together we are, here and now.

A Single Dawn

Softly breaks the morning light,
Whispers of a new delight.
Colors dance upon the sky,
A promise as the night draws nigh.

Birds awaken, sing their tune,
In the glow of rising June.
Every shadow fades away,
In the warmth of golden ray.

Gentle breezes brush the trees,
Nature sways with perfect ease.
Moments linger, sweet and clear,
A single dawn, a day to cheer.

Hope is born with every hue,
A canvas, bright, and fresh and new.
Step outside, embrace the day,
Let your dreams come out to play.

Time will flow, and seasons change,
Yet this dawn will not feel strange.
In our hearts, we hold it tight,
A treasure of the morning light.

Pause and Reflect

In the rush, take a moment,
Breathe in deep, feel the potent.
Life's a tapestry, so vast,
Each thread woven from the past.

Thoughts like rivers gently glide,
In this stillness, we abide.
Mindful space, where worries cease,
In this calm, find your peace.

What's your truth, what do you seek?
In the silence, hear the meek.
Listen close, the heart will speak,
In this pause, life feels unique.

Every choice that brought you here,
Celebrate, hold it dear.
Lessons learned, both hard and sweet,
In this moment, feel complete.

So when time feels fast and bleak,
Remember this gentle peak.
Pause and reflect, just breathe in,
Let the journey now begin.

Each Tick of Time

Time, a river, ever flows,
In its currents, wisdom grows.
Moments pause, then swiftly wane,
All that's lost will still remain.

Each tick holds a memory dear,
Echoes of laughter, whispers near.
Capture joy, embrace the now,
With every tick, take a bow.

Seasons change, the clock's unkind,
Yet in its hands, we often find
Beauty seated in the hours,
Life's a dance among the flowers.

Cherish both the highs and lows,
In their wake, our spirit grows.
Time may rush, but we can choose,
To live in love, to never lose.

So bind your heart to every chime,
Celebrate each tick of time.
In its passage, stories unfold,
Whispers of the brave and bold.

The Light of This Hour

Golden beams of sunlight spill,
In this moment, time stands still.
Feel the warmth upon your face,
Embrace the gift of this sweet place.

With each heartbeat, dreams take flight,
Guided softly by the light.
Here and now, we're fully seen,
In the present, calm and serene.

Gentle whispers fill the air,
Nature sings a tune so rare.
In this hour, we are free,
To simply be, to just see.

Let the shadows fade away,
In the glow of this bright day.
Hope ignites, a spark divine,
In this hour, truly shine.

So gather strength from every ray,
In the warmth, we'll find our way.
Hold this light, let love empower,
Live fully in the light of this hour.

Now is Where We Begin

In the dawn's soft glow, we rise,
Dreams awaken in clear skies.
Every heartbeat, a chance to start,
With open minds and eager hearts.

Footsteps whisper on the ground,
In silence, new hopes abound.
Together we chase the morning light,
Embracing each day, holding it tight.

With every breath, we start anew,
Painting our worlds in vibrant hue.
In the moment, let worries cease,
For now is where we find our peace.

Each step forward, we carve our way,
Unfurling dreams, come what may.
In the journey, the magic sings,
Now is where our spirit clings.

Let not the past define our scope,
In this moment, we ignite hope.
Hand in hand, let's face what's near,
Now is where we conquer fear.

Moments that Matter

A shared laugh by the old oak tree,
Simple joys, just you and me.
Time stands still in that warm embrace,
In fleeting moments, we find our place.

The flutter of wings, a bird in flight,
Sunset whispers, painting the night.
A soft caress of summer air,
In moments that matter, we lay bare.

Each heartbeat echoes in the still,
Gathering memories, strength, and will.
A glance exchanged, no words required,
In love's quiet moments, we're inspired.

Let's seize each fragment as it flows,
In fragile hours, deep magic grows.
In laughter, tears, we carve our way,
Moments that matter shape our day.

As seasons change, we hold them tight,
In every day, find pure delight.
For life's a tapestry, rich and bright,
In moments that matter, we find our light.

Captured in a Blink

A child's laughter fills the air,
Echoing softly everywhere.
Sunbeams dance on morning dew,
Captured in a blink, just me and you.

Time flows swiftly, like a stream,
Chasing shadows, chasing dreams.
A fleeting glance, a wink exchanged,
In a heartbeat, love is arranged.

The world spins fast, yet we hold still,
In these minutes, we find our thrill.
Moments glimmer, bright and rare,
Captured in a blink, love laid bare.

Life's a collection of little things,
The joy and peace that memory brings.
So let us cherish what we create,
For in a blink, it could turn to fate.

Hold close the whispers of each day,
In blink of an eye, we slip away.
Grasping time, we embrace the past,
Captured in a blink, our love will last.

Seize the Day's Light

Morning breaks with a golden hue,
Awakening dreams, fresh and new.
In every moment, treasure the shine,
Seize the day's light, let your heart align.

With every challenge, rise and stand,
Together we journey, hand in hand.
The horizon calls, a vivid sight,
In every heartbeat, we find our might.

Let laughter carry us through the air,
In joyful whispers, we find our care.
As shadows merge and daylight dances,
Seize the day, embrace the chances.

Time is fleeting, like waves on sand,
Molding moments, life's gentle hand.
We are the authors of our own tale,
In the day's light, we shall prevail.

So rise and shine, let ambitions soar,
In each new dawn, there's so much more.
Embrace the journey, love what's in sight,
For every day brings its own light.

The Weight of One Sunrise

The dawn breaks soft and bright,
A canvas washed in light.
Colors dance upon the sky,
As the world begins to sigh.

Gold and crimson paint the hues,
Whispers carried by the views.
Each moment, a treasure found,
In the silence, peace abound.

Birds awaken, songs take flight,
Chasing shadows into night.
Every shimmer, every ray,
Guides us gently on our way.

The weight of promises untold,
In every sunrise, dreams unfold.
The day ahead, a fresh embrace,
With hope and joy, we find our place.

In the light, we stand renewed,
With gratitude and a heart imbued.
The weight of one sunrise to bear,
In its glow, we find our prayer.

Today as an Open Book

The pages turn, the story flows,
In each line, a new path shows.
With ink of dreams and hopes so bright,
We write our tales in morning light.

Every moment, fresh and clear,
A chapter filled with joy and fear.
We scribe our laughter, pain, and grace,
In the margins, we find our place.

As whispers of the past unfold,
Present moments yet untold.
In every paragraph we weave,
Today, we choose to dream, believe.

The ink may fade, the words may blur,
But in our hearts, the feelings stir.
Today as an open book, we see,
The beauty of what's meant to be.

So let us write with all our might,
Fill each page with pure delight.
Today a canvas, fresh and bright,
An open book, a future's light.

A Journey of Instants

In a heartbeat, life expands,
Moments stitched by time's own hands.
Each second, a flicker of flame,
In the tapestry, no two the same.

With echoes of laughter, whispers blend,
A river of time that twists and bends.
Instants like stars, they shine and fade,
In memories made, our hearts are laid.

We wander through life's crowded maze,
In the dance of time, we softly gaze.
Every glance, each fleeting sigh,
A piece of the puzzle, a reason why.

Through corridors of dreams we roam,
Finding the warmth that feels like home.
A journey crafted, moment by moment,
In every instant, a new component.

We hold the now, we cherish the past,
In the embrace of time, we're unsurpassed.
A journey of instants, brief yet grand,
Forever etched in life's gentle hand.

Embraced by the Moment

In stillness lies a gentle grace,
Time slows down, we find our space.
Embraced by now, in softest light,
We breathe it in, everything feels right.

The rustling leaves, a quiet sigh,
Nature whispers, we can fly.
In the here and now, we flow,
As the world around us begins to glow.

Moments stolen from the rush,
In this quiet, feel the hush.
Every heartbeat, a sacred tune,
We sing along beneath the moon.

Embraced by the moment, we stand tall,
With open hearts, we welcome all.
In tenderness, we find our truth,
In this dance, the spirit's youth.

So let us linger, let us stay,
In the present's warm array.
For in each moment, joy does bloom,
Embraced by love, we cast aside gloom.

A Moment to Breathe

In stillness, find your peace,
A whisper of the breeze,
Take a moment, let it flow,
Feel the rhythm, let it grow.

With each breath, release the weight,
In silence, learn to wait,
Close your eyes, let thoughts drift,
Find the calm, a precious gift.

Nature speaks in subtle ways,
In the light of golden days,
Pause to listen, soak it in,
Let your journey now begin.

A puddle reflects the sky,
Clouds drift gently, passing by,
In the moment, life unfolds,
Secrets waiting to be told.

So take a deep and gentle breath,
Embrace the life, encircle death,
For in this space, you truly see,
A moment to just be free.

Whispers of the Present

Time softly calls your name,
A flicker, never the same,
In the now, a treasure waits,
Open hearts can change the fates.

Gentle raindrops kiss the ground,
Listen close, a soothing sound,
Every heartbeat, every sigh,
A reminder not to fly.

In the present, find your song,
A melody that feels so strong,
Every moment, crystal clear,
Whispers linger, ever near.

Let go of worries, let them fade,
In this space, be not afraid,
Hold the warmth of fleeting time,
In the now, you'll feel the rhyme.

Breathe in deeply, feel the grace,
Every second leaves a trace,
In the whispers, life abounds,
In the moment, love surrounds.

Embracing the Now

The clock ticks on, the world spins round,
In the now, let joy be found,
Every heartbeat, every way,
Embrace the gift of today.

Moments dance like flickering light,
Paint the canvas, pure and bright,
With each dawn, new paths unfold,
Stories in the silence told.

Feel the breeze, it speaks your truth,
Awaken dreams, revive your youth,
In the now, be true, be bold,
Live the life that you behold.

The sun dips low, shadows entwine,
Capture peace, let spirits shine,
Every second brings delight,
Hold on tight, embrace the light.

Morning whispers, evening sighs,
In this moment, realize,
Life's a gift, don't let it go,
Embracing the now, let love grow.

Today's Gentle Choice

A single leaf upon the stream,
Gently drifting, like a dream,
Today holds magic in its hand,
Choose to walk on golden sand.

Every smile, a chance to share,
Kindness lingers in the air,
With each choice, let love arise,
In the echoes, find the prize.

Turn your gaze toward the sky,
Watch the clouds and let them fly,
Today's whispers softly say,
Choose to shine bright in the gray.

In every heartbeat, find renewal,
Life's sweet song, a soft jewel,
As the sun begins to rise,
Today's gentle choice, be wise.

So take a breath, step forth with grace,
Embrace the world, find your place,
Let today be all you seek,
In each moment, let love speak.

This Hour's Embrace

In the quiet corners of time,
Whispers of light begin to chime.
Each second a gift, soft and clear,
Wrapped in a hug that draws us near.

Moments like petals drift and fall,
Painting the canvas, hear their call.
Embrace the hour, let it unfold,
Stories of warmth and tales untold.

Time dances lightly, shadows tease,
Gentle reminders in the breeze.
With every heartbeat, we align,
In this sweet hour, your hand in mine.

Laughter lingers, time stands still,
Echoing dreams, a shared thrill.
As stars wink softly in the night,
This hour's embrace, a pure delight.

The Sweetness of Now

Moments glisten like morning dew,
Each heartbeat pulses, fresh and new.
In this instant, time feels slow,
Savor the sweetness, let it flow.

Bright smiles flourish, shadows fade,
In the warmth of love, we wade.
Every glance a gentle tease,
A gift wrapped in simple ease.

Candles flicker, stories blend,
Holding hands, forever friends.
The sweetness of now, pure and bright,
Painting our lives in hues of light.

Breathe in deeply, let worries cease,
In this moment, find your peace.
With every laugh, with every sigh,
We share a treasure that won't die.

A Tapestry of Moments

Threads of laughter, woven tight,
Stitching memories in the night.
Colors vibrant, stories twine,
A tapestry of love divine.

Each moment a bead, a story spun,
Crafted together, two become one.
In the loom of life, we intertwine,
Creating a pattern, uniquely fine.

Weaving dreams with every thread,
In the fabric where hopes are spread.
Glimmers of joy, shadows of pain,
Stitching it all, love's sweet refrain.

A tapestry unfolds, rich and vast,
Embracing our future, honoring past.
In every fold, a memory glows,
A story of us, a tale that grows.

The Color of This Moment

Brush strokes of laughter splash the air,
Vivid hues that dance with flair.
Every heartbeat paints the scene,
In the color of what has been.

Golden rays cascade like dreams,
Illuminating life's bright beams.
In this moment, shades entwine,
Crafting a palette, yours and mine.

Cobalt skies and emerald fields,
Beauty that nature lovingly yields.
In every glance, a canvas new,
The colors of life, rich and true.

Moments collide, a vibrant trace,
Painting our hearts in time and space.
With every breath, the colors blend,
In this moment, love transcends.

The Calm of the Current

Beneath the whispering trees,
The water flows so free,
Soft ripples kiss the shore,
Inviting us to be.

A gentle breeze does play,
As sunlight starts to ray,
The world feels light and bright,
In nature's warm embrace.

Each moment flows like dreams,
In silken, silver streams,
We lose ourselves in peace,
Where nothing's as it seems.

Time drifts on a sigh,
Like clouds that wander by,
In this serene expanse,
We learn to let it lie.

Here love is endlessly,
Like waves that hug the sea,
In the calm of the current,
We find our spirit's key.

The Dance of Today

The sun paints skies with gold,
Awakening the bold,
Each heartbeat feels like rain,
In stories yet untold.

Moments spin and twirl,
As dreams begin to swirl,
With every breath we take,
We dance within the whirl.

In laughter shared with friends,
As joy never ends,
We learn to sway with grace,
Where the music blends.

The rhythm beats so strong,
In life, we all belong,
Together in the now,
We move and hum along.

Each step is filled with light,
A spark, a pure delight,
In the dance of today,
We shine through every night.

In the Midst of Chaos

A storm brews in the skies,
As thunder rumbles by,
Yet in this wild uproar,
A quiet heart can fly.

The world may spin around,
With chaos all around,
But stillness lives within,
Where peace can be found.

Fierce winds do whip and howl,
As shadows skulk and growl,
Yet love can light the path,
A guiding, gentle fowl.

In turmoil, we can stand,
With steadiness at hand,
Embracing all the storm,
And finding where we land.

So let the tempest rage,
We'll write a different page,
In the midst of chaos,
Our hearts can be the stage.

The Overflow of Now

The present swells and flows,
With secrets yet to show,
Each moment brims with life,
In the overflow of now.

Time whispers soft and sweet,
In rhythm with our feet,
As dreams and hopes collide,
In this dance, we repeat.

A canvas stretched so wide,
Where colors swirl beside,
Every heartbeat sings loud,
In joy we must abide.

With every breath, we feel,
The magic that is real,
Awash in endless waves,
A love we will conceal.

In the pulse of the day,
We learn to simply play,
In the overflow of now,
We soar and drift away.

A Sunrise of Possibilities

The dawn unfolds its golden light,
A canvas fresh, a hopeful sight.
Each ray a mark of dreams to chase,
In every corner, a warm embrace.

With whispers soft, the world awakes,
New journeys born with every break.
Possibilities bloom in the sky,
As hearts take flight, as dreams comply.

A palette rich, a vibrant hue,
Every moment, something new.
The future bright, a path to trace,
Awaits the bold in this vast space.

Beneath the sun, we stand in awe,
Embracing life without a flaw.
Each second holds a chance to seize,
A sunrise wrapped in gentle breeze.

A symphony of hope resounds,
In every heart, a life abounds.
With every heartbeat, let us strive,
With open arms, we come alive.

The Heartbeat of Today

In rhythm soft, the world breathes slow,
A dance of time, a gentle flow.
With every tick, we find our place,
In this moment's warm embrace.

The sunrise paints the sky so bright,
Awakening dreams to share the light.
Around us swirls the vibrant sound,
Each heartbeat echoes, life profound.

We move through hours, like rivers run,
Collecting memories, one by one.
In fleeting moments, joy is found,
In laughter shared, our spirits abound.

Let today be a canvas wide,
Where hopes and wishes coincide.
With every beat, with every sigh,
We carve our path beneath the sky.

The heartbeat of today whispers clear,
A reminder that we're ever near.
In this dance, let's celebrate,
The beauty of now, it's never late.

The Clarity of This Instant

Time pauses here, a breath, a glance,
In this still frame, we take a chance.
The noise of life melts away,
Revealing truths that come to stay.

With open eyes, we start to see,
The beauty of simplicity.
This moment calls, it sings our name,
In clarity, we find the flame.

No burdens weigh on hearts today,
Just gratitude for the light's display.
Each heartbeat whispers, 'Now's the time,'
In every breath, a subtle rhyme.

We stand united, souls aligned,
In the embrace of all we find.
The clarity shines, a precious gift,
A tapestry where spirits lift.

Let's cherish now, this fleeting grace,
In every smile, in each embrace.
The clarity of this instant glows,
In timeless truth, our essence flows.

Today's Gentle Refuge

In the hush of morning light,
We find a space, a world so bright.
Today unfolds like petals fair,
A gentle refuge, free from care.

The whispers of the trees surround,
In nature's arms, peace can be found.
With every step, the heart can soar,
In quiet stillness, we explore.

Moments linger, soft and sweet,
In simple joys, our souls retreat.
The warmth of sun, the song of birds,
A symphony that needs no words.

In laughter shared with friends so dear,
We build a space where love draws near.
Today's embrace, a soft caress,
In every heartbeat, we are blessed.

Let time stand still, let worries cease,
In this sanctuary, we find peace.
Today's gentle refuge, a sacred space,
Where hearts intertwine in sweet embrace.

A Diary of This Hour

In the stillness of time, I write,
Moments captured, pure and bright.
Whispers of thoughts, they softly flow,
Pages turned, as the night glows.

Each heartbeat a tick, a steady pace,
In shadows long, I find my place.
Reflections linger, the ink does gleam,
A diary of now, a waking dream.

Memories waltz in the quiet air,
Each word a treasure, woven with care.
The hour unfolds like petals in bloom,
A sanctuary found in this gentle room.

Soft echoes of laughter fill the space,
In this diary, I leave my trace.
Time breathes softly, a fleeting kiss,
In every moment, I find my bliss.

So I pen my heart, let it fly,
In the pages, my spirit sighs.
A diary written under starlit skies,
Holding the hours where my truth lies.

Echoes of the Present

In the pulse of now, we find our way,
Echoes of laughter dance and play.
Moments woven with gentle grace,
The present whispers in this space.

A heartbeat shared, a glance that speaks,
In the silence, the soul seeks.
Fragments of time, they shimmer bright,
In the embrace of the fading light.

Each breath is a note in the song of life,
As joy and sorrow intertwine in strife.
Echoes linger in the evening air,
In the tapestry of moments we share.

With every heartbeat, the world spins round,
In the present, true beauty is found.
A symphony played on the strings of fate,
In echoes of now, we contemplate.

So let us savor this fleeting hour,
In the whispers of time, we find our power.
With hearts wide open, we learn to see,
The echoes of the present set us free.

A Canvas of Now

Brush strokes of light, a vibrant hue,
Creating a masterpiece, just for you.
Colors blend in a soft embrace,
On this canvas, I find my place.

Splashes of laughter, a dash of tears,
Captured moments throughout the years.
Every detail tells a tale sublime,
A canvas of now, transcending time.

In the silence, the visions bloom,
Crafted dreams in every room.
Wisps of history in shades of gold,
A story unfolds, waiting to be told.

As the sun sets, the colors shift,
In twilight's whisper, the spirits lift.
With each stroke, the world aligns,
On this canvas of now, our heart entwines.

So let us paint with vibrant tones,
In the art of living, we find our bones.
With every brush, let our souls ignite,
Creating a canvas, our true delight.

Sipping the Sweetness of Today

In the morning light, I take a sip,
Sweet nectar flowing, a gentle drip.
Moments linger in the steaming cup,
Sipping the sweetness, I soak it up.

Each flavor dances on my tongue,
As the day awakens, fresh and young.
The warmth surrounds, a tender glow,
In this sweetness, my spirit flows.

With every sip, the world ignites,
Dreams and hopes take glorious flights.
In the quiet, I find my way,
Sipping the sweetness of today.

As time drifts softly like a breeze,
In every moment, my heart finds ease.
With gratitude pouring from my soul,
Today's sweetness makes me whole.

So here's to life, the highs and lows,
In every cup, the beauty grows.
Sipping slowly, let joy replay,
In the sweetness of now, we'll forever stay.

Holding the Present

In the stillness of now, we find our peace,
Moments unfold, like petals they release.
Time, a gentle river, flows with grace,
We anchor ourselves, in this sacred space.

The past whispers soft, the future unknown,
Here we stand grounded, never alone.
Each heartbeat a whisper, each breath a song,
Holding the present, where we all belong.

Let worries dissolve, like mist in the light,
In this fleeting moment, everything feels right.
We gather our thoughts, like stars in a night,
Embracing this instant, with hearts burning bright.

In laughter and silence, the joy radiates,
Life's simple pleasures, oh, how it celebrates.
Every glance a treasure, every touch divine,
In holding this moment, our spirits align.

Now is a garden, where dreams take flight,
Painted in colors, vivid and bright.
With gratitude blooming, we take a breath,
In the heart of the present, we dance with no end.

A Flicker of Light

In the dark, a glimmer, a spark in the night,
Hope flickers softly, guiding our sight.
Through shadows and doubt, it rises above,
A beacon of warmth, a whisper of love.

With every small candle, we gather as one,
Illuminating paths until the day is done.
Each flicker a promise, each glow a prayer,
In the heart of the night, we find solace there.

The flicker expands, casting ripples of grace,
Uniting our spirits in this sacred space.
Together we journey, through valleys and peaks,
In the light of our love, it's connection we seek.

Embers are memories, warmth from the past,
Guiding us forward, a bond that will last.
A flicker of light leads us through the storm,
In unity, we stand, in each other, we're warm.

So hold on tightly, to that flicker within,
For in the darkness, our journey begins.
With courage declaring, through silence and sound,
A flicker of light, in each heart to be found.

Celebrating This Breath

Inhale the moment, feel it alive,
Exhale your troubles, let your heart thrive.
With each sacred breath, a new chance unfolds,
A dance of existence, in stories untold.

The rhythm of life, it pulses with grace,
In the silence we find, our own perfect place.
Every whispering wind, every rustling leaf,
We celebrate this breath, in joy or in grief.

As time passes gently, we learn to embrace,
The beauty of living, the warmth of this space.
In gratitude, we find, like stars in the night,
Celebrating this breath, it feels so right.

Together we gather, in laughter and tears,
In a tapestry woven from hopes and from fears.
Each moment a treasure, each heartbeat a gift,
In this dance of existence, our spirits uplift.

So take a deep breath, let your essence ignite,
Celebrate the journey, each shadow and light.
In the pulse of your being, let your heart sing,
In celebrating this breath, we find everything.

The Essence of This Minute

In the essence of now, we gather our souls,
Time's fleeting nature, it constantly rolls.
Each second a gem, shining ever so bright,
We savor the whispers, the warmth of the light.

Moments like diamonds, precious and rare,
In stillness, we breathe, feel the love in the air.
The clock ticks softly, yet we stand content,
In the essence of this, where our spirits are bent.

As minutes unfold, like petals in bloom,
We dance with the present, dispelling all gloom.
Find beauty in silence, in echoes of grace,
In the essence of this minute, we carve out our space.

Each tick a reminder, to cherish and hold,
In the warmth of connection, our stories unfold.
Together we weave, in the tapestry fine,
The essence of this minute is purely divine.

So take a brief pause; let your heart intertwine,
With the magic of now, in this moment, we shine.
In the essence of this minute, forever we'll stay,
Embracing each heartbeat, come what may.

Vows to the Morning

In silence, I greet the day anew,
With whispers of promise, soft and true.
The sun peeks over the hills so shy,
Painting the sky, as daylight draws nigh.

Each ray a vow, a warmth to share,
Breathing life into the cool, crisp air.
I pledge to cherish each fleeting hour,
Embracing the dawn, its radiant power.

Birds sing sweet tales of hope and grace,
Their melodies weaving through time and space.
With each heartbeat, I'm filled with cheer,
These morning moments, so precious and dear.

The dew-kissed flowers begin to bloom,
Filling the world with their sweet perfume.
Together we dance, this day we claim,
In the light of morning, nothing's the same.

With open arms, I welcome the light,
A canvas of dreams, bold and bright.
Vows made in the morning, to infinity extend,
As the day unfolds, my spirit can mend.

Threads of Living Color

In gardens where colors intertwine,
Each petal whispers a story divine.
Threads of living color, vibrant and free,
Woven by nature, a tapestry.

The sun spills gold on the earth below,
As shadows stretch long, they start to flow.
Blossoms in a dance, they sway and spin,
Celebrating life that thrives within.

With hands in the soil, I plant my dreams,
Each seed a promise, bursting at the seams.
Watered by laughter, nurtured by care,
Threads of connection, binding us there.

In every hue, I find pieces of me,
Reflections of joy, and days carefree.
In this vibrant world, let hearts take flight,
Together we bask in the colors of light.

The evening draws near, the hues start to blend,
As day turns to night, we'll still transcend.
With threads of living color, we'll weave our fates,
In the fabric of moments, love resonates.

The Diary of the Instant

Each second writes tales in shadows bright,
A fleeting moment, captured in light.
The diary of the instant, pages unfold,
Whispers of memories, both fragile and bold.

Time dances lightly on delicate toes,
A brief window where the heart knows.
With every heartbeat, a story is spun,
Inscribed in the ether before it is done.

Smiles shared over coffee, laughter in air,
These tiny treasures, beyond compare.
Each flicker in time holds the essence of now,
In the diary's embrace, I make my vow.

A glance or a touch, ephemeral bliss,
The joy of connection, a gentle kiss.
Each instant a page that turns with grace,
In the book of forever, I find my place.

So let me be present, alive in this space,
With gratitude woven through time's sweet embrace.
The diary of seconds, a tapestry spun,
Weaving our stories, two hearts beat as one.

From Dawn to Dusk

From dawn's first light to twilight's embrace,
The day unfolds in a soft, gentle pace.
With whispers of colors, the sky takes flight,
Painting the world with warmth and delight.

Flowers awaken, stretching to the sun,
As shadows retreat, the day has begun.
Moments of stillness, hurried and fast,
From dawn's soft kiss to dusk's quiet cast.

Children's laughter fills the air with glee,
Chasing the light, wild and carefree.
The sun rides high, like a king in his throne,
Marking the hours with a glow, overgrown.

As daylight dims, the stars start to peek,
The sky transforms, dark velvet and sleek.
From colors so bright to the cloak of the night,
The day sings its lullaby, fading from sight.

From dawn to dusk, life's moments unspool,
In the tapestry of time, we each play the fool.
With hearts wide open, we dance in the glow,
Embracing the journey, wherever we go.

The Art of Temporary

In the fleeting glow of twilight's embrace,
We find beauty in moments, a delicate trace.
Like whispers of wind, they dance and then fade,
Art lies in the echoes, in memories made.

Each sunrise brings colors that shimmer and play,
Yet soon they dim down as the night steals the day.
We gather the fragments, hold them near tight,
Knowing they vanish, yet bask in the light.

Life's portrait is painted with strokes quick and bold,
A canvas of laughter, a tapestry told.
In the blink of an eye, everything shifts,
Embracing the transient, the heart truly lifts.

Like a fleeting glance shared between strangers we meet,
Every heartbeat counts, even bittersweet.
In the art of the moment, we grasp what we can,
For life's vivid strokes paint the heart of a man.

So cherish the now, the brief and the fine,
In each fleeting second, there's magic divine.
For in the art of temporary we weave,
A legacy found in the love that we leave.

One Day, One Breath

One day stands before us, bright and clear,
A promise of moments we hold so dear.
Each breath that we take is a step on our way,
Molding our future with choices today.

The sun peeks through clouds, a warm radiant glow,
Whispers of hope in the gentle winds blow.
In the hush of the morning, we find our own ground,
In the heart of the silence, new dreams can be found.

Let's dance in the sunlight, laugh, sing, and play,
Embrace the present, let worries drift away.
Each heartbeat a rhythm, a pulse of delight,
A reminder that living is our greatest right.

One step leads to another, a path we must tread,
In the tapestry woven with threads finely spread.
Today's our canvas, our story unfolds,
With each stroke we take, new destinies mold.

So let's treasure this moment, for soon it will pass,
Each second a gift, like dew on the grass.
One day, one breath, we create with our hands,
Carving our fate as the universe expands.

Today's Canvas Unfurled

A fresh canvas awaits, colors wild and bright,
Brushes dipped gently, igniting the light.
With each stroke of the day, we bring forth our dreams,
In today's vast expanse, hope silently beams.

The dawn whispers softly, a call to create,
Telling our story, reminding us fate.
Emotions like pigments, they blend and they swirl,
In the masterpiece forming, our lives start to twirl.

With laughter and sorrow, we paint with intent,
Every hue tells a tale, each moment well spent.
The sun shines its warmth as we splash on the blue,
In today's canvas, our souls shine anew.

Let's capture the essence of all that we feel,
In the dance of our lives, reality reveals.
Every flick and each flourish brings us to thrive,
Creating a vision, we blossom alive.

When the day fades to twilight, we'll glance at our chart,
The artwork of living, each piece holds a part.
Today's canvas unfurled, a journal of grace,
In the gallery of moments, we find our true place.

A Small Eternity

In the hush between heartbeats, a silence unfolds,
In moments so brief, a universe holds.
A glance and a smile, time pauses to breathe,
In the smallness of now, eternity weaves.

The fragrance of flowers, a song on the breeze,
Whispers of yesterday stir with such ease.
In the dance of the fleeting, we savor the day,
A tapestry woven in laughter's array.

Like grains of fine sand slipping softly away,
Each second a treasure we cannot delay.
We gather the fragments of time's gentle flight,
In this small eternity, our hearts feel delight.

We chase after shadows, we reach for the stars,
In the depths of the moment, we find who we are.
So hold on to the flashes that brighten our soul,
In the smallness of eternity, we find ourselves whole.

When the hours drift softly, like whispers on air,
In the smallest of moments, we're unbound, we're rare.
For in every heartbeat, love's resonance sings,
Creating a legacy from the joys that life brings.

Moments of Radiance

In the glow of dawn's embrace,
Soft whispers dance in grace.
Colors bloom, the shadows fade,
Each breath, a promise made.

Sunlight spills on quiet streams,
Awakening the sweetest dreams.
Nature sings a vibrant tune,
Cradled by the afternoon.

With every heartbeat, time suspends,
Heartfelt laughter, warmth descends.
Moments cherished, held so dear,
In this light, all feels clear.

Underneath a painted sky,
As clouds of amber gently fly.
Hope ignites with every glance,
In the warmth of this sweet dance.

So let us cherish what we find,
In every heartbeat intertwined.
For in these rays, life's truth is shown,
In moments of radiance, love has grown.

A Quiet Invitation

Amidst the hush of falling night,
A gentle call, soft and light.
Whispers beckon, come and roam,
In this stillness, find your home.

Step into shadows, feel the peace,
Let your worries find release.
Through the silence, secrets play,
In the dark, dreams find their way.

Stars above begin to shine,
With every twinkle, hearts align.
Hold the moment, let it grow,
In quiet corners, love will flow.

Every rustle, every breeze,
Carries softly through the trees.
The night awaits, a gentle guide,
An open heart is all you need inside.

So linger here, don't rush away,
In this serene and sacred sway.
A quiet invitation, softly made,
In every heartbeat, memories laid.

The Road Not Taken Today

A fork appears beneath my feet,
Two paths lie waiting, bittersweet.
One whispers close, the other beckons,
In silence deep, my heart reckons.

With every step, I weigh my choice,
In quietthoughts, my inner voice.
What lies ahead, what should I seek,
A journey new, a chance to speak.

Leaves of autumn whisper low,
Guiding steps where dreams may grow.
Yet, choices linger in my mind,
The road ahead, a treasure to find.

What if the trail is one less worn?
A chance to rise, a chance reborn.
In every moment, let me stay,
To seize the road not taken today.

For life unfolds in choices small,
Each turn through shadows, we recall.
In the journey, I shall find,
The path of meaning, intertwined.

Floating on Today's Breeze

The morning whispers soft and clear,
A gentle touch, a breath so near.
Leaves are dancing, skies so wide,
Floating softly on the tide.

Clouds drift by in lazy grace,
Time slows down, we find our place.
A moment captured, hearts alive,
In the warmth where hopes can thrive.

Sunbeams flicker, shadows play,
Every moment calls to stay.
Trust the wind to lead us on,
Floating through to the dawn.

Let the worries drift away,
In this magic of today.
With open arms, we embrace the shine,
Floating softly, your hand in mine.

So breathe in deep, feel the air,
In this dance, we softly share.
Floating on today's sweet breeze,
Life unfolds with gentle ease.

Daily Choices

Each dawn brings paths anew,
In choices, lives unfold.
With courage, we pursue,
The stories yet untold.

Moments gray, moments bright,
We shape them with our hands.
In silence or in fight,
We weave our own demands.

The whispers in the breeze,
Guide us where we should go.
With every heart that sees,
A seed of hope can grow.

In laughter or in tears,
We stand before the gate.
Each choice dispels the fears,
To craft a perfect fate.

So walk the paths ahead,
Embrace the joy or strife.
In choices lightly tread,
To paint the hues of life.

Daily Blessings

Awake to morning light,
A gift we can embrace.
With every breath so bright,
We find our sacred space.

The laughter of the day,
A melody so sweet.
In small and grand display,
Each blessing feels complete.

The smile of a kind friend,
The warmth of hands held tight,
In love, our troubles mend,
Transforming dark to light.

A moment's peace to hold,
In chaos and in calm.
These blessings, worth more than gold,
Bring comfort like a psalm.

So cherish what you find,
In every passing glance.
In gratitude combined,
We join the joyful dance.

Shimmering Crumbs of Time

In fleeting hours we tread,
Like breadcrumbs on a path.
Each moment left unsaid,
Can spark a soft new math.

The laughter shared today,
A glimmer in the past.
In memories, we play,
Those shimmering moments cast.

Let not the days rush by,
For time is a gentle stream.
In stillness, we can fly,
And breathe our waking dream.

The sunset's golden hue,
Carves shadows on the ground.
In twilight's final cue,
New stories can be found.

So gather all the light,
That dances in your mind.
With heart and soul ignite,
The treasures left behind.

The Heartbeat of a Day

With sunrise, life awakes,
Pulsing in vibrant sway.
In every heartbeat's stakes,
We craft the light of day.

The rhythm of the hours,
A dance both slow and fast.
In quiet, gentle powers,
We're anchored to the past.

The laughter in the air,
The sigh of evening's calm.
In moments that we share,
We find our common balm.

So pause to feel the life,
In echoes soft and true.
Though time may cut like knife,
The heartbeat's always you.

A pulse that leaves no trace,
Yet carves the world so wide.
In each contained embrace,
The essence of our stride.

Fleeting Glimmers of Thought

A whisper in the night,
A thought can softly glow.
Like stars that twinkle bright,
In shadows, seeds can sow.

The mind's wild, restless flight,
Can capture dreams untold.
In silence, sparks ignite,
With wisdom wrought from gold.

Each fleeting glimpse we chase,
Can lead to wider skies.
Within this sacred space,
Our understanding flies.

As feelings rush like streams,
We navigate the flow.
In every thought that beams,
A deeper truth may show.

So hold these glimmers close,
For they can change the way.
In thoughts that gently pose,
We find life's grand ballet.

Milton Keynes UK
Ingram Content Group UK Ltd.
UKHW021159251124
451300UK00024B/147